*Like streamers, rivers in Mt. McKinley
National Park twist and cross.*

# Alaska
## AND
# Yukon

# Alaska
## AND
# Yukon

*Text by John Goddard*
*Principal Photography by Ulrich Ackermann*

**Discovery Books**

Published in Canada by
Discovery Books, Toronto


*Photo Credits:*

*Ulrich Ackermann:*
cover, 2, 9 (above), 12 (above) 13–20, 22–23, 25–35,
37–42, 44–52, 53 (above), 54–69, 71–79, 81–89, 93, 137

*Jerg Kroener:*
53 (below)

First Light Associated Photographers:

*Brian Milne:*
9 (below), 11 (left), 12 (below), 21, 36, 43, 80, 94, 95, 98,
99, 100–101, 104–105, 106, 119, 120–121, 124, 125 (above)

*Patrick Morrow:*
6–7, 11 (right), 90–91, 96–97, 102 (above), 107–113,
115–117, 118 (left), 122, 123, 125 (below), 126–130,
132–133, 134 (above), 135, 139, 140–144

*Paul von Baich:*
10, 102 (below), 103, 118 (right), 131, 134 (below),
136, 138

ISBN 0-919493-98-X

Design: Heath and Associates
Printed and bound in Italy

6 5 4 3 2 1

# Contents

# Introduction

The northwest corner of North America is an unusual part of the world, with peculiar appeal. Few people live there. And of those who arrive from elsewhere, few stay more than a year or so. The median age in Anchorage, Alaska's largest urban center, is under twenty-four; every three or four years close to half the population turns over. The land and people of the Alaska, U.S.A. and Yukon Territory, Canada are divided by an international boundary, different currencies, different flags, and to some extent different modes of living. But they are joined by latitude, geography, a common road system and a common attitude about their place in the world.

Northerners, whether American or Canadian, share a sense of remoteness. The North is no longer isolated, but people living there still feel removed from rest of the world, which they call "the Outside." They could travel in a few hours to Washington or Ottawa, their nation's respective capital cities, but they speak as though their federal governments were on the moon. Insecure about their meagre voting power, Alaskans disparage "the lower 48", and Yukoners disparage "the South." But the sense of remoteness also makes Northerners feel special. A person doesn't have to live long in the North before developing proprietary feelings towards the place. The region is still raw enough and the people so few that everyone has a chance to be recognized, feel important, make a mark.

Winter turns street life in Alaska and the Yukon into an elaborate game of peek-a-boo. Pedestrians bustle incognito along sidewalks in extreme cold, peeping at one another from within fur-trimmed parka hoods. Each scrutinizes the other for a tell-tale moustache, a familiar nose profile, an identifiable curve to the mouth. It is the only way to pick out friends and colleagues for passing salutations until parka colors, mittens or distinctive footwear can be memorized. Sometimes entire bodies fade in and out of view, momentarily engulfed by billowing clouds of exhaust created by pickup trucks left idling at curbside so they won't freeze. Occasionally entire towns are lost, shrouded in ice fog and veiled from the low, emasculated winter sun, which by mid-winter is out for less than four hours a day in the main urban centers of Anchorage and Fairbanks in Alaska, and Whitehorse in the Yukon.

Hooded clothing, billowing vapor, darkness and fog combine to create an unearthly, shadowy world. It is the world of absolute winter in the Far North. Absolute winter is the season in which Northerners cease to think in terms of degrees of temperature, just as passengers at sea do not consider the varying depths of the water. It is a giddy season at the outset; the otherworldliness is a novelty. The winter clothes are as amusing as Hallowe'en disguises. Frost cloaks every tree in sparkles, and snow paves over potholes and garbage. The North is again unmistakably northern and residents are

The rich brown coats of the moose cow
and her calf protect them from cold.
Moose enjoy browsing on twigs and
leaves in wooded areas.

The pika is the smaller cousin of the
rabbit and the hare. It lives mostly in
the mountains and feeds on leaves and
twigs.

again true Northerners. A sense of community congeals around them.

The night winter sky often flows with greenish illumination: the aurora borealis, or northern lights. Constantly in motion, ever-changing in intensity, the aurora sometimes streams like vapor from a high-flying plane, sometimes swirls like cigarette smoke, sometimes descends to create what looks like a giant set of organ pipes. On rare occasions the light cascades like a waterfall, turning pink at the ends and making a distinct, eerie, swishing sound. Dinner parties are interrupted when a guest spots a particularly stunning display. Everyone rushes to the window or puts on a parka to step outside. Drinkers who happen out of a bar and look up at such moments are moved to vulgar exclamations of wonderment.

Eventually the winter days start to drag. "We're in the tunnel," Alaskans sometimes say, referring to the darkness. Winter clothes, once novel, get merely cumbersome. Office workers at the coffee machine talk about how they've been having trouble getting out of bed lately. They are drowsy again by mid-afternoon and nod off after supper. Lethargy spreads

like influenza. By March, colleagues and neighbors are on each other's nerves. Those who can't afford Hawaii begin to drink a little more. Frozen patches of blood accumulate outside the most popular bars.

Finally, in April, there is plenty of sunlight again. The ice is still firm, perfect for moving on the land by dog team or snow machine. After Easter, native villages nearly empty as entire families head out to spring camps to hunt moose, and to trap muskrat and beaver. Office workers become speedy again, and get by on little sleep. With summer come flowers, mosquitoes and tourists. The northern mystique becomes less pronounced. Yet the northern summer is not like summer elsewhere. The days stretch out. On June 21, the longest day of the year, Fairbanks gets 22 hours of daylight. The northern air blowing over vast meadows and alpine glaciation picks up a rarefied aspect. The season is all the more poignant for being short.

It is, indeed, a land unlike any other, infinitely beautiful and haunting, as much for the people who choose to live there as for those who live to the south.

**Left:**
*A male spruce grouse fans his tail and neck feathers. In mating season, grouse use such displays, along with various movements and calls, to attract females.*

**Above:**
*Kobuk sand dunes are a surprising feature of the Alaska landscape. They form a part of the only desert in Alaska and one of the northernmost sand deserts in the world.*

**Opposite:**
*Cold, calm waters echo the image of surrounding mountains.*

Left:
Crab fishermen check the size of their catch.

Preceding pages:
A hazy backwater in Sitka Sound. Sitka was once the administrative center for the Russian fur traders.

Opposite:
A black bear and her cub fish for salmon by a rushing stream. Gulls stand by waiting for leftovers.

Left:
*The least sandpiper nests in tundra
marshes and grassy ponds.*

Preceding pages:
*Southern slopes of mountains near
Portage, Alaska, catch the rays of the
low-lying winter sun.*

Opposite:
*Colorful fireweed blooms in the Yukon.*

# Alaska

# 1
# *The Last Frontier*

The Indians call it "Denali" — the Great One, the High One, the Mighty One. A young Princeton graduate prospecting in 1896 renamed it Mount McKinley, after William McKinley who had just been named Republican nominee for United States president. That name stuck, but the mountain is still great, high and mighty, soaring 20,300 feet into the sky. It is the highest mountain in Alaska. It is gigantic and angular and mysterious, often shrouded in its own vapor. It is an apt symbol for Alaska itself.

Mountains are what give Alaska so much of its raw majesty. They are the extensions of two mountain ranges running parallel from California — the Rocky and Pacific cordilleras. The Rockies, sweeping north and west, become the Mackenzie Mountains in Yukon and finally the Brooks Range in Alaska. These are not particularly high. In contrast, the Pacific cordillera is a solid wall of granite bastioned by the six highest peaks, the largest glaciers and the only remaining active volcanoes in North America. This mountain chain, called the Coast Mountains in British Columbia, becomes the St. Elias Mountains in Yukon, then the Alaska Range of which Mount McKinley is part, and finally the Aleutian Range, which sinks into the Pacific Ocean just short of Asia. Running between the two mountain ranges from southern Yukon to the Bering Sea in western Alaska is the Yukon River — the last major North American river to be discovered by white explorers.

The variety of topography — coast, mountains, central basin — implies a variety of climates. Juneau, the state capital, has the most untypical climate of northern cities, tucked into a mountain valley of the Alaskan Panhandle on the Pacific coast. There is no permafrost, the winter temperature seldom goes much below freezing, and it rains 220 days a year. Winds reach speeds of more than 200 miles per hour. On the other hand, Alaska's northernmost settlement of Barrow, 330 miles north of the Arctic Circle on the coast, conforms more closely to the image of the frozen North. For more than 60 days in winter the sun does not rise, and temperatures drop to 40 and 50 degrees Fahrenheit below zero for weeks.

Alaska is home of the bald eagle, found elsewhere in any numbers only in British Columbia. The bald eagle is the Mount McKinley of birds: rawly majestic and white-capped. Its broad wing span and sheer size make it a stirring sight as it glides towards the upper branch of a Sitka spruce, stretches its feet forward, flaps to stalling speed and sets itself heavily down on the perch to have a look around.

Alaska is also known for its king, or chinook, salmon, which average 20 pounds each and die heroic martyr deaths in answering their reproductive urge — one of the wonders of nature. After five to seven years at sea, they migrate to the mouth of the Yukon River and start upriver in early June to the spawning beds of

Preceding pages:
*Massive Mount McKinley is the highest point in North America. Called "Denali" by the Indians, the peak is named after William McKinley.*

Opposite:
*Grizzly bears are active during the summer months. In the fall, they enter a dormant period which can last half the year.*

the various tributaries where they were born. They move in schools according to which spawning bed they came from, the salmon from the Porcupine tributary, for example, swimming separately from those of the Nisutlin. Night and day they swim against the current, covering as much as 30 miles a day, a feat demanding stamina and a navigational skill that continues to mystify biologists. By the time they reach the spawning grounds, they are scrawny, battered, infected and exhausted. The female begins digging a hole in the gravel with her tail, to a depth of about six inches. She releases hundreds of red, sticky eggs while the male at her side releases a milky cloud of sperm. The functions are repeated several times until as many as 12,000 eggs are expelled. Then the adults die, spent, and the eagles swoop in to clean up.

In terms of big game, the Alaska grizzly bear best symbolizes the untamed wildness of the North for most people.

It is as swift as it is massive, as swift as a race horse. Its sense of smell is highly refined but its eyesight is poor. To focus on something it is curious about, it stands on its hind legs and squints, a gesture often misunderstood as preparation for attack. When truly angry, the bear stands four feet on the ground, head down, ears cocked and jaws chopping.

Alaskan native people for the most part, and many old-time Alaskan residents, still rely on hunting, fishing and trapping to sustain themselves: salmon, moose, caribou, whale, wolf and fox, depending on where they live in the state. But there is an increasingly urban dimension to Alaska as well. Anchorage is the largest city, holding half the population of the state. It grew out of a tented construction camp established in 1915 as headquarters for the Alaska Railroad. But not until the Second World War, when the army established its Alaskan defense

headquarters and when commercial air routes made Anchorage a supply center, did the city begin to boom. Now it is the administrative center for oil-exploration firms and for the trans-Alaska pipeline — running from Prudhoe Bay on the Arctic coast to Valdez on the south coast. Although the commercial heart of the state, Anchorage is sealed off from the rest of Alaska by water on one side and by mountains on the other. It is separated from the rest of the state, as well, by its urban concerns, more commonly associated with cities to the south. Streams and lakes in the immediate area have long since been fished out. The moose have left. A bush plane is needed for access to the wilderness and its wildlife. Yet a reminder of Alaska's true majesty is easy to come by, even in the middle of the city, for in the distance stands Mount McKinley, the Great One.

Above left:
*Primarily a fish eater, the bald eagle has suffered because its diet is frequently contaminated with pesticides. Only in the rain forests of Alaska and British Columbia have its numbers remained undiminished.*

Left:
*The morning sun catches a young Dall's mountain sheep. The only wild white sheep, Dall's feed on mountain slopes in early morning and late afternoon.*

Opposite:
*Reds and yellows paint the landscape near Mount McKinley in a brief flash of autumn color. Mount McKinley National Park was established in 1917 and is home to an abundance of wildlife.*

Above:
*An Eskimo hunter with the head of a caribou he has hunted. Hunting still constitutes an important part of the Eskimo way of life.*

Right:
*A young sled dog gnaws a bone.*

Preceding pages:
*Harbor seals rest on an ice floe. These mammals are deft swimmers but are slow and awkward out of the water.*

Opposite:
*Through the centuries, this river has cut through the cliffs that now loom above it.*

Left:
*A true northern creature, the hawk-owl stays awake during the long summer days to hunt lemmings and mice. In winter, its main diet is birds.*

Preceding pages:
*The glacial ice sloping down to the frigid waters of Glacier Bay has been carved into strange shapes by wind and weather.*

36

Opposite:
*Sand dunes at Kobuk form an unexpected pattern of sand and ice. The Kobuk River valley desert lies in the northwestern corner of the state above the Arctic Circle.*

Canada geese come north for the summer. They nest along marshes and ponds and lay three to eight eggs. When hatched the young birds will accompany their parents south for the winter.

Preceding pages:
The caribou's magnificent antlers are shed each winter. Each spring a new set grows.

Opposite:
During their spawning runs, when salmon are slow-moving and weak, they are easy prey for fishermen and bears.

Above:
*Red-throated loons are found high in the Arctic. Loons' legs are set far back on their bodies, making them nearly helpless on land.*

Right:
*Nocturnal and ferocious for its size, the weasel changes from brown in summer to a winter white.*

Opposite:
*Winter descends on the lakes and streams of the Brooks Range, the highest mountain range within the Arctic Circle.*

# 2
# The Fabled Land

The idea of walking overland from the Soviet Union into the United States sounds extraordinary today, but at one time Asia and North America were joined. A land bridge about 1,000 miles wide stretched between what now are Siberia and Alaska, 30,000 to 40,000 years ago. The bridge allowed nomadic peoples from Asia to migrate into North America through the interior lowlands of Alaska and the Yukon Valley. At Old Crow in northern Yukon, anthropologists have found bits of serrated caribou bone—almost certainly used as tools—dating back more than 25,000 years.

Descendants of some of the peoples who made the crossing are found in Alaska today. Collectively they are referred to as native peoples, or Alaska Natives, and are further distinguished as Inuit, Aleuts and Athapaska Indians. The Eskimos, also known as Inuit, live mostly along the coasts of the Bering Sea and the Arctic Ocean—along migratory routes of the marine mammals they once hunted in kayaks and umiaks. They lived in houses of driftwood, antlers, whale bones and sod. The Aleuts, also reliant on fish and marine mammals, and once famous for tightly woven baskets, inhabit the eastern Aleutian Islands and the Pribilof Islands farther north. The Athapaskans, once almost wholly dependent on great caribou herds, inhabit the wooded interior. All native groups lived an austere and hard-working existence dependent on hunting and fishing. So it is ironic that Europeans came to look upon Alaska as a storehouse of glamorous forms of wealth: furs, gold and, most recently, oil.

On June 4, 1741, Vitus Jonassen Bering, a Dane in the service of the Russian navy, set sail from the Siberian peninsula of Kamchatka to explore the sea that now bears his name, and to find out whether a land bridge still existed between the two continents. It was his second such mission, and in the course of it he discovered vast colonies of sea otters, animals prized by the Chinese for their luxurious fur. Word of the discovery spread. Independent Russian traders known as promyshleniki plundered the Aleutian Islands and southern Alaska for fur, often enslaving or slaughtering the Aleuts in the process. Prior to the arrival of the Russians, an estimated 20,000 Aleuts inhabited the Aleutian Islands; by the end of the eighteenth century about 2,000 were left. The formation of the Russian-American Company in 1799—modelled after the Hudson's Bay Company in Canada, and with a fur-trade monopoly in Alaska granted by the czar—stemmed the worst of the excesses against local inhabitants.

This was small consolation for the sea otters. Between 1775 and 1825, the Russians slaughtered 200,000 sea otters for their pelts. Sitka, on the Alaska Panhandle, became the center of operations,

*Snow covers the ghostly remains of an arctic village.*

flourishing also as a port of call for American ships bound for China. Sitka became a town of board sidewalks and neat wooden houses with window boxes full of flowers. It had a fine Orthodox cathedral, a library and a shipyard. Its aristocratic naval administrators spoke Slavic-accented French.

Years of unrestrained slaughter eventually brought the sea otter to the brink of extinction. New peltries were needed if the Russian-American Company was to survive. Russian explorers began to reconnoiter the Bering Sea coast in earnest, looking for a great river to the interior that Indians had spoken about. The explorers found the mouth of the Yukon River and established a trading base. Then Russian traders penetrated the interior, finding rich fur supplies and groups of Indians willing to do business. All this time, however, the Russians never tried to develop Alaska as an outpost of empire. To them, Alaska was a vast fur farm.

Attempts to colonize the place were half-hearted, apart from the necessity of setting up an administration center like Sitka, and supply bases such as St. Michael at the Yukon River mouth. At no time did Russian settlers number more than 1,000.

In contrast, the British and Americans were as possessive as they were aggressive. Wherever fur traders went, missionaries and settlers seemed to follow. American merchant sailors competed with the Russians on the northwest coast, gaining control over coastal trade in the Russian-American treaty of 1824. British fur traders pushed northwest through British Columbia and Yukon, then boldly into Alaska to compete with the Russians head on. The Russians backed off, saving face in 1839 by leasing southwest Alaska to the Hudson's Bay Company.

The British kept pressing. The Hudson's Bay Company sent one of their most determined traders to compete with the Russians on the Yukon River in the

Alaskan interior. His name was Robert Campbell, an able if dour Scot, and his assignment was rife with hardship and danger.

One particularly fractious incident took place August 20, 1852. Campbell had just returned to his base of Fort Selkirk on the Pelly River in what is now Yukon Territory, bringing back supplies that included a live cow. He and three others were cutting grass for the cow in a meadow near the fort when 27 Indians of the Chilkat nation landed in rafts on the riverbank brandishing guns. The Chilkat had acted as middlemen between the Russians downriver and the Indians of the upper Yukon before Campbell had come along, and were upset over losing their monopoly. At first the Chilkat did nothing but hang around the fort frightening the British traders. But the next morning, they grew bolder, thieving openly, growing more rambunctious, and finally routing the British traders from the fort. Campbell was fired at and, at one point, an Indian lunged at him, accidentally stabbing a dog that had run between the two men. Campbell and his group retreated, returning the next day to find everything, as Campbell put it, ''smashed into a thousand atoms.''

In 1867, the United States bought Alaska from the Russians for $7.2 million, and the territory was touted as America's ''last frontier.'' The acquisition was not particularly popular at the time; even supporters justified it not for commercial reasons but as an act of friendship with Russia, and as being of potential strategic value. In any case, the purchase stirred the imaginations of frontiersmen like Leroy McQuestern, Alfred Mayo, George Wilkenson and Arthur Harper—all adventurers and explorers who lived by fur trading and prospecting, and who helped open up the land to settlement through a series of gold strikes in the 1880s and 1890s.

*Opposite:*
*A Russian Orthodox church.*

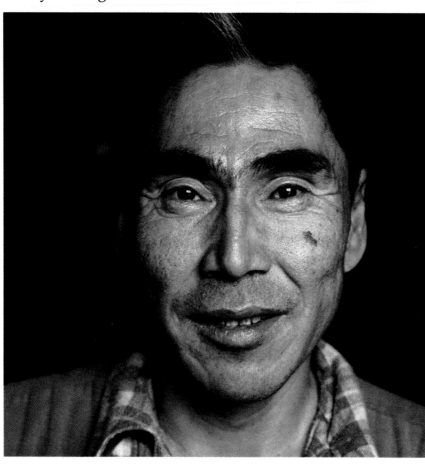

*An Eskimo man. The Eskimos, or Inuit, were once the only people to live north of the treeline in the Arctic. They are believed to be the descendants of migrant Asians who crossed the Bering Strait on a land bridge.*

*A young Athapaskan woman. The Athapaskan people lived inland and were once almost wholly dependent on the great caribou herds that roamed the region.*

Left:

*A young girl of Russian descent stays close to her home in Alaska. The state once belonged to the Russians, but they never settled it extensively or developed it. In 1867, they sold it to the Americans for $7.2 million—a purchase that was considered foolish at the time.*

Below:

*Two women in traditional Russian costume wait while a third changes a tire on their van. Alaska's population is a melting pot of native peoples and descendants of settlers—American, Chinese, Japanese, Filipino, as well as Russians, who were probably the first white arrivals.*

*An elderly American-Russian relaxes on his porch.*

*Young girls in traditional dress run down their village street.*

**Above:**
*A beaver dam partially blocks the flow of a small creek.*

**Opposite:**
*The golden hues of fall touch the vegetation of the Wrangell Mountains. The heights of these mountains are mostly covered by a large ice cap which feeds large valley glaciers.*

**Right:**
*The beautiful arctic crocus is one of many flowers that cover the northern landscape in the spring.*

*Weeds have taken root on the roof of this abandoned arctic church.*

*Old, rusty bells guard a small Russian graveyard on a bluff overlooking English Bay.*

Opposite:
*Lush summer greenery contrasts with the snow-capped peaks at Katmai National Monument. In 1912, one of the world's most violent volcanic eruptions took place here.*

Preceding pages:
*A fishing boat returns home to Sitka at sunset.*

*A totem pole at Sitka features the sophisticated and stylized art form of the west coast Indians. The animals represent helping spirits, and the poles themselves serve a number of functions. A large collection of totem poles at Sitka National Monument commemorates the stand of the Tlingits against early Russian settlers.*

Preceding pages:
*The still waters of Glacier Bay reflect the surrounding scenery. Glacier Bay National Monument is one of three national monuments in Alaska. It features magnificent fjords as well as slowly retreating glaciers.*

Opposite:
*An approaching storm seems to tumble over the mountains in Mount McKinley National Park.*

*Pieces of an old steam engine lie strewn near Nome as if scattered by a giant.*

*A decaying boat creates an atmosphere of melancholy at Kobuk.*

Opposite:
*Built during the Gold Rush, this old cabin in McCarthy may have been deserted as hope for riches failed.*

Fishermen haul in their catch of crabs. Fishing is a major part of Alaska's economy, along with mining, timber and petroleum. As well as crab, the boats bring in halibut, herring and shrimp. The unregulated fishing of Soviet and Japanese fleets has recently posed a threat to the industry and to the ecology of the northern waters.

Preceding pages:
Small wooded islands in Sitka Sound are dwarfed by the Coast Mountains. These islands are part of the chain that stretches from Vancouver in the south and protects the Alaska Panhandle and the British Columbia coast.

Opposite:
The end of a good day's fishing: nets and fish hang to dry in Kiana on the Kobuk River in northwestern Alaska.

# 3
# A New Challenge

In 1968, the discovery of an oil-and-gas reservoir off the north coast of Alaska at Prudhoe Bay was announced, the largest find of oil and gas in North America. The discovery set off the greatest boom in Alaskan history. Throughout the 1970s, construction of an oil pipeline from Prudhoe Bay to Valdez dominated the state economy, promising large oil revenues for years to come.

A decade later, in 1978, 170,000 square miles of Alaska wilderness was withdrawn from mineral or oil development— an area larger than California. The U.S. Congress and President Jimmy Carter, while not interfering with the Prudhoe Bay development, were recognizing the value of Alaska's wilderness. Carter designated as national monuments such areas as the Yukon River Valley, a coastal area known as the Bering land bridge, Glacier Bay and the St. Elias Mountains. "Among the treasures to be preserved are the nation's largest pristine river valley, the place where man may first have come into the New World, a glacier as large as Rhode Island and the largest group of peaks over 15,000 feet in North America," Carter said at the time. Also protected were the forests of Misty Fjords and Admiralty Island in southeastern Alaska, that otherwise would have been cut, at least in part, and the land opened to mineral exploration.

If there is a basic tension in Alaska politics today, it is over the way in which Alaska might proceed: of preservation versus development, of wilderness versus the bulldozer. It is easy to understand why other Americans might want the wilderness preserved; pristine areas are rare in the world now, especially areas of such scenic beauty as Alaska. But there is support for preservation within Alaska, too, because rapid development of the oil fields proved too much too fast for places like Fairbanks and Anchorage. Old-time Alaskans suffered severe disruptions: a population influx, inflation and a general proliferation of urban evils that many people had originally come to Alaska to escape.

As Alaskans feel their way to some kind of balance on the development issue, they must also come to grips with how the needs of Alaska natives can be accommodated. In 1971, to open the way for the Trans-Alaska Pipeline, the U.S. Congress passed the Alaska Native Claims Settlement Act, celebrated at the time as generous to the native people and a model for aboriginal claims elsewhere. The settlement awarded the natives a billion dollars and 44 million acres of land. The problem was that the money was assigned to native corporations created for the purpose, obliging native groups to try to go into business, and the land was divided and assigned to different groups and bands, creating border disputes. Now the settlement looks like a bad deal for the natives. Most of the native corporations are on the verge of bankruptcy. There is a danger that native lands will have to be

*The lights on an oil tower at Prudhoe Bay glow eerily. Oil was discovered here in 1968, and the find set off the greatest boom in Alaskan history. The trans-Alaska pipeline now runs from Prudhoe Bay to Valdez on the south coast of the state.*

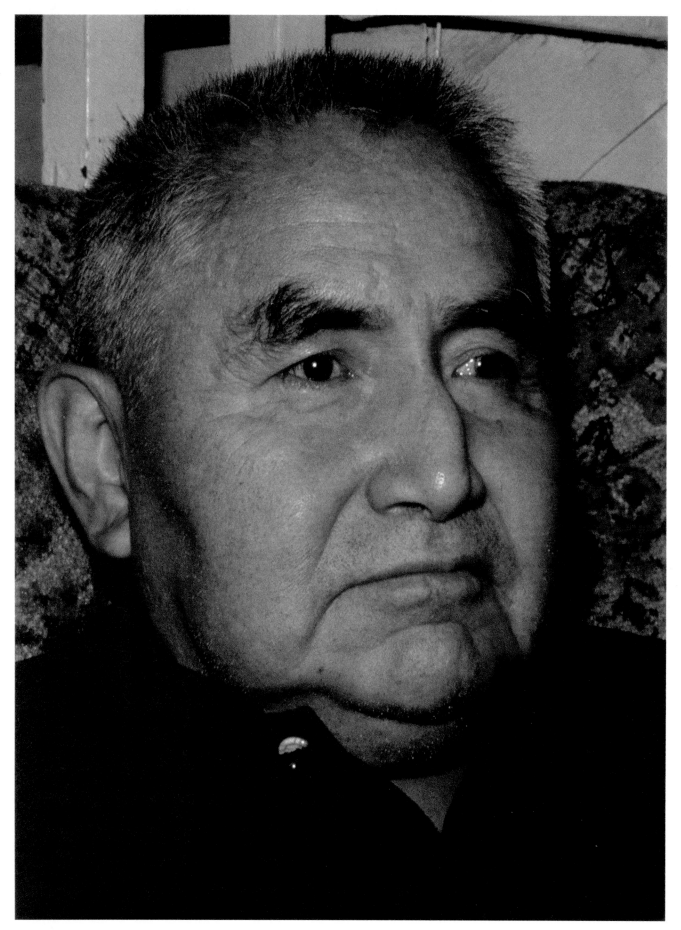

*A Tlingit chief. The coastal Tlingits lived by fishing and hunting. An artistic and fierce people, they roamed as far as Puget Sound in ocean-going war canoes.*

sold off to pay the debts. If that happens, native villagers throughout Alaska would lose the subsistence economy on which most of them still depend for their livelihood and collective identity.

Thomas Berger, a former Canadian judge who studied the problems of Alaska natives for two years, reporting his findings in 1985, predicted Alaska natives would lose their lands if Congress does not act to change the legislation. He implored the U.S. federal and state governments to act and issued a dire warning on Alaska's future if they do not. ''Without its Native villages, without the subsistence way of life, Alaska would not be Alaska,'' Berger warned in his report, *Village Journey*. ''Without Native villages, this wild and rugged country would become an antiseptic wilderness . . . If they lose their land, Alaska Natives who now live in villages would drift to the cities in ever larger numbers and become a financial burden on the state. Moreover, the presence in urban surroundings of an embittered Native population would make impossible the achievement of a partnership between Natives and non-Natives that is still possible in Alaska.''

Top:
*The ancestors of these Aleut girls survived the arrival of the Russians in the eighteenth century. When the Russians came to the Aleutian and Pribilof islands in search of furs, they enslaved and slaughtered many Aleuts, decimating the population.*

Left:
*An Eskimo girl and her grandmother in Kiana wear contrasting clothes — a modern ski jacket and a traditional parka.*

*Its large feet and shaggy coat help the caribou to survive the arctic cold. The males use their antlers for fighting in the breeding season in October.*

Preceding pages:
*Ridged and scored, a glacier in Glacier Bay National Monument moves with ponderous slowness to the sea.*

*The discovery of oil brought prosperity and hope to Alaska. It also brought a threat to the wilderness and the end to an old way of life for many.*

*A male king eider stands in a shallow pond. Flocks of thousands of eiders come to the Arctic each spring. In fall the males leave first, followed by the females.*

Preceding pages:
*A large chunk of ice breaks off Columbia Glacier and falls into the sea.*

Opposite:
*The arrival of winter makes graphic patterns on the tundra.*

*A husky awaits its master outside a bar in Nome.*

Preceding pages:
*The setting sun lights the peaks of the Wrangell Mountains above Silver Lake. These volcanic mountains rest on sedimentary and igneous rocks.*

Opposite:
*Low water levels form a beach along a river near Denali.*

*Hoping for a handout, gulls follow a commercial crab boat as it plies the offshore waters.*

*A commercial fishing boat in its slip.
Many Alaskan fishermen operate as
small independents, working the inshore,
coastal fishery in boats such as this one.*

Following pages:
*As the sun sets, the lights of Anchorage
come on. The city, which now holds
half the population of Alaska, started in
1915 as a construction camp for the
Alaska railroad.*

Yukon

# 1
# Arctic Wilderness

"This pamphlet will protect you from the bears," says the woman at the Parks Canada trailer. She means the pamphlet tells how to avoid encounters with bears, but we tease her, unfolding the pamphlet into a bear shield, then rolling it into a stubby bear knife.

The Parks Canada woman laughs at the gags; she is used to tourists. Every summer, more than 10,000 people stop at her trailer at the foot of Sheep Mountain, on the perimeter of Kluane National Park. They stop to ask about the park, an awesome wilderness in the southwest corner of Yukon Territory embracing the spectacular St. Elias mountain range with its large ice fields, alpine meadows and Canada's highest peak, Mount Logan (19,520 feet). People also stop to ask about Sheep Mountain, a favorite of Dall's sheep — mountain sheep with distinctive curled horns. There are more than 4,500 Dall's sheep in the park and Sheep Mountain is a good place to find some of them. "I don't know where they are today," the Parks Canada woman says. "Maybe around the other side." And we are off.

The day is sunny and hot, with a cool breeze blowing from the icefields, out of view to the southwest. We climb steadily, eagerly, and attain considerable elevation before pausing for a view. "Majestic grandeur," one companion says. A panorama of jagged, snow-capped peaks catches the eye first, then the sweeping mountainsides in shades of blue, mauve, green and yellow, in patches of varying intensity

determined by the shadows of scattered clouds. But no sheep.

Further on, we come upon mounds of overturned earth — evidence of a bear. In mid-summer, bears dig up arctic ground-squirrels and a plant called hedy sarem, which has a root rich in carbohydrates. We get out the bear pamphlet. "In most cases," it says, "a bear will move off if it knows you are coming. So be seen and be heard." One of us dangles the car keys as we walk. Further on, we see bear tracks. We start singing.

Late in the day, as we are starting back down, having seen no bears and no sheep, an eagle crossing the sky leads our gaze to an upper ridge of the mountain. And there they are: sheep, five of them, stepping gingerly about on thin, knobby legs, rooting into rock crevices for vegetation, their distinctive horns plainly visible.

A casual encounter with the Yukon wilderness easily becomes an extraordinary afternoon: expansive mountain scenery, alpine air, exotic animals and a whiff of danger. There is a pristine quality to much of the Yukon that appeals to visitors and residents alike. The Yukon is big-game country. It has brown, black and grizzly bears, moose, caribou, mountain goats, Dall's and stone sheep — also a few elk and muskox, protected from hunters. Nearly 5,000 hunting licences are sold to residents every year and more than 500 to outside hunters who must be accompanied by a licensed guide. The fishing is

Preceding pages:
*In the Ogilvie Mountains, a scene as bright and rich as any tapestry.*

92

Opposite:
*A group of Dall's ewes rests in the sunshine. Dall's sheep are wary of predators and prefer alpine meadows.*

good, too. Arctic grayling, lake trout and northern pike are the most common species, while ardent fishermen try for rainbow trout, dolly varden, whitefish, salmon and inconnu. Between 15 and 20 per cent of Yukon native people still fish for subsistence in spots used for centuries, both in summer and in winter through the ice.

There is also a wide variety of birds, including bald eagles, hawks, trumpeter swans, northern phalaropes, ovenbirds, long-tailed jaegers and rare peregrine falcons. Fireweed is the territorial floral emblem, a plant that lights up entire hillsides in July in glowing purple-pink. Other common flowers are two types of orchids, strawberry blite, arnica, Jacob's ladder, forget-me-nots, bluebells and the yellow arctic poppy — nearly 500 plant species altogether.

To be close to nature, some Yukoners live a semi-bush existence — a cabin in the woods without electricity or running water — though close enough to town to pick up mail twice a week and see friends. Others live a semi-town existence, taking off to the cabin on weekends and for extended periods during the summer. Almost everyone at least owns a pair of hiking boots. And although the capital of Whitehorse is in many ways a staid civil-service town, most residents have favorite spots they wander off to in the surrounding hills.

Top:
*Grass tussocks and flowers color the land far into the distance.*

Left:
*Two newly hatched rock ptarmigans huddle near their mother. The rock ptarmigan changes color with the seasons. In summer its plumage is a mottled dark brown-gray. In winter it is entirely white except for a partly black tail and black markings above the eyes of the male.*

Opposite:
*The antlers of the bull moose can reach up to seven feet from tip to tip.*

Left:
*A pair of young great horned owls.*
*These birds are found in the north up*
*to the treeline.*

**Preceding pages:**
*Snow-clad peaks near Mt. Vancouver in*
*Yukon Territory.*

Holding a fish in her mouth, a female arctic tern surveys the beach where she will nest. To avoid the dark northern winter, these terns migrate to the waters near Antarctica.

Appropriately named for its colorful legs, the lesser yellowlegs often submerges its whole head when chasing after small fish and aquatic insects in shallow water.

Top:
*Bright yellow arctic poppies catch the summer sun.*

Right:
*Fireweed, the territory's floral emblem, blooms in front of a log cabin in Teslin.*

Preceding pages:
*A grizzly bear sends a spray of drops as it shakes the water from its fur.*

Opposite:
*Dew-laden soapberries brighten the arctic landscape.*

Above:

*A hoary marmot blends in well with his rocky habitat. Marmots hibernate for up to eight months and may lose up to half their autumn weight by spring.*

Right:

*Two red fox kits at play. Born early in the spring, foxes are cared for by their parents for about six months.*

Preceding pages:

*A flock of whistler swans stand and swim in shallow water. Whistler, or tundra, swans come to the tundra lands of the Arctic each year to breed.*

106

*Icy water rushes over lichen-covered rock in the Tombstone Ramparts in the Ogilvie Mountains.*

*Wispy clouds are reflected in a pond in the Richardson Mountains.*

Preceding pages:
*Shadows of clouds glide across an emerald lake in the mountains.*

Opposite:
*The bounty of the north: a catch of chinook salmon lies on the banks of the Teslin River. After five to seven years at sea, these salmon migrate to the mouth of the Yukon River. They return to the tributary where they were born where the females lay their eggs, which are then fertilized by the males.*

# 2

# History

The quest for fur opened Yukon to outsiders, but gold put it on the map. The most famous strike happened August 17, 1896. Three prospectors from the village of Carcross near the Yukon-B.C. border, down on their luck, were felling trees for lumber at Rabbit Creek, a tributary of the Klondike River near the Arctic Circle. They were George Carmack, originally from California and his brothers-in-law Skookum Jim and Tagish Charley. While off on his own one day, Skookum Jim knelt for a drink of water and saw chunks of gold in the creek bed. The others joined him later and they, too, saw raw gold lying thick between slabs of bedrock, ''like cheese sandwiches,'' in Carmack's words. ''Then as near as I can remember,'' Carmack later recalled, ''three full grown men tried to see how big damn fools they could make of themselves. We did a dance . . . composed of a Scotch hornpipe, Indian fox trot, syncopated Irish jig and a sort of a Siwash Hula-Hula.'' Carmack renamed the creek Bonanza. Then he and Charley rafted for a day down to the gold mining town of Forty Mile on the Yukon River, population 300. There they registered their claims and set off the Klondike gold rush.

The rush was local at first, attracting prospectors already in the area, some of whom had been advancing towards the Klondike since the 1870s. Once there, they spent a hard winter, many of them becoming extraordinarily wealthy while continuing to live wretched lives in huts and lean-tos, withstanding appallingly low temperatures on a diet of baked beans. In July, 1897, several dozen of the miners headed south, arriving in two boatloads, one day apart, in Seattle and San Francisco. One man, Clarence Berry, staggered off the steamboat in Seattle bearing $130,000 worth of gold.

America was in the grip of a depression at the time, and although almost all the best Klondike claims had been staked, thousands of people headed north with visions of wealth. Most caught steamers up the British Columbia coast to the Alaskan port of Skagway, the population of which shot from one to 12,000 in less than a year. Those continuing north had to cross the rugged Coast Mountains, either by the Chilkoot Pass or the White Pass. And cross they did: in long lines from horizon to horizon, bent double under the weight of supplies or urging their horses and mules up the steep, frozen terrain. It is estimated 3,000 beasts dropped dead on the White Pass alone, yet loss of human life was minimal. From the mountains, the gold-seekers floated down a series of rivers and lakes to Dawson, which was taking shape on the mud flats where the Klondike and Yukon rivers meet. Between 15,000 and 20,000 people reached Dawson at the height of the rush in 1898, and almost as many the year before.

Some accounts of the Klondike gold rush make much of the gambling and prostitution and throwing about of gold.

Preceding pages:
*Mist settles around an abandoned dredge in the Klondike. These machines once churned along river and creek beds picking up gravel, separating out the gold, and spitting out the remains.*

Opposite:
*Pale winter sunlight glints on the industrial area of Whitehorse. Now the capital of Yukon Territory, the city was founded as a temporary stopping point at the head of navigation of the Yukon River.*

*A modern car is reflected in the window of a typical early Dawson building. At the height of the Gold Rush in 1898, 20,000 people lived in Dawson. Three years later, the population was just over 9,000. The city now survives mostly on tourism and is maintained as a historical site.*

Above left:
*A small gold mining operation. Over the years many methods have been used to separate gold from the gravel and sand into which it has settled. Some independent operators remove topsoil with bulldozers; then the exposed gravel is washed through sluices. The heavy gold particles sink and separate out.*

Above right:
*Mail awaits the inhabitants of Dawson. Named after G.M. Dawson, the leader of the expedition that explored the region in 1887, Dawson became the capital of the Yukon Territories in 1898. In 1951, Whitehorse took over the position.*

And certainly there must have been rowdy times amid the toil and hope and desperation. But about the only out-and-out lawlessness was in the Alaskan town of Skagway, called the toughest town in America at the time, and controlled by the infamous Soapy Smith—a bland, smiling hooligan who prospered through gambling, prostitution, hijacking, theft and murder. He was finally gunned down on the Skagway docks.

In Canada, life was well ordered. The federal government responded to the gold strike by promptly sending in more than 100 men from the North-West Mounted Police. By the end of 1898 the force numbered nearly 300. Dawson was laid out in uniform blocks by federal surveyor William Ogilvie, with avenues exactly 66 feet wide. No gold-laden pack train was ever hijacked leaving the Klondike. And all gambling joints and brothels were closed Sundays in accordance with Canadian law. By 1900, a social elite in Dawson City had coalesced around the commissioner, or territorial governor, and even the shanty-town suburb of Louse-town had telephones and electricity.

Perhaps the most outstanding Canadian personage of the era was NWMP

Superintendent Sam Steele—Soapy Smith's opposite. Steele supervised the mountain passes at the Yukon River headwaters dispensing advice, collecting duty and making sure the more than 30,000 stampeders that passed there were properly equipped. He required every stampeder to come supplied with 1,150 pounds of food. ''We had seen that the sick were cared for,'' Steele reported later, ''had buried the dead, administered their estates to the satisfaction of their next-of-kin, had brought in our own supplies and means of transport, had built our own quarters and administered the laws of Canada without one well-founded complaint against us.'' Most of the gold-seekers were Americans, but the police presence helped Canada retain the territory when the Alaska-Yukon border was officially established in 1903.

The gold boom ended with a whimper. Dawson had 20,000 people in 1898—not counting surrounding camps and villages. By 1901, the population had dropped to 9,142. By 1921, it had dropped to 975. ''Dawson was a bizarre community to be raised in,'' says Pierre Berton, the Canadian broadcaster, author and Klondike historian, born there in 1920. ''It was a ghost town falling apart. There were no airplanes, no sun for six weeks of the year, no fresh fruit or vegetables for eight months. But there were a lot of interesting people, a lot of people still around who had made it over the Chilkoot Pass.''

The next stampede was into the southern Yukon, but not for gold. During the Second World War, U.S. President Roosevelt feared a Japanese invasion of America through Alaska and the Canadian northwest. He ordered a military road be built from Dawson Creek, B.C., to Fairbanks, Alaska. And the Canadian government quickly approved. The scale of the project was enormous: 1,500 miles of road. The expense was great: $140 million, a fortune then. The hardships were many: mosquitoes, muskeg, loneliness and fear of actual battle on what became known as ''the road to Tokyo.'' There were no environmental hearings, and no cross-examinations by government-funded citizens groups, just the courage and brawn of men working to deadline. The U.S. Army Corps of Engineers, with some Canadian help, finished the bulk of the work in less than nine frantic months in 1942.

The Japanese never came, but the arrival of the U.S. army was like an invasion to the people already there. Whitehorse was transformed from a town of 500 people to a construction hub for 30,000 workers. ''I was head of the post office,'' Laurent Cyr recalled in 1982 at a 40th-anniversary ceremony in Whitehorse. ''With no advance warning, 10,000 soldiers landed here over three days, all wanting letters from home.''

The native people were more or less overrun by the boom through disease, illegitimate children and the bulldozing away of a traditional way of life. But the experience wasn't all bad for at least one Indian employed by the U.S. engineers as a guide. ''I led the road past a lot of little lakes,'' Johnny Johns admitted in a short speech at the 40th-anniversary ceremony, explaining why the original road had so many bends and curves. ''I liked to go fishing in the evenings.''

*Opposite:*
*Conifers and distant mountains: a view from the Klondike Highway.*

*Below left:*
*The tint of minerals and the random cracks in the mud create an interesting texture in a dried river bed.*

*Below right:*
*Built by the Athapaskan Indians, these spirit houses in Champagne are on top of graves. They are filled with tea, cups and other necessities to help the spirit on its journey to its final resting place.*

Preceding pages:
Autumn's colors are muted by the season's first snow along Top of the World Highway.

*The Anglican church in Moosehide was dedicated to William C. Bompas, a missionary who established a boarding school for native children in Carcross.*

**Above:**
*A beaver paddles across the pond it has formed by damming a northern stream. These large rodents feed largely on the bark of trees.*

**Right:**
*A climatic anomaly, the Carcross desert is the northernmost extension of the arid interior plateau that, farther south, forms the Great Basin Desert.*

**Opposite:**
*The grizzly bear survives on a varied diet that includes large animals like caribou as well as berries and grubs.*

**Following pages:**
*Dempster Highway crosses vast unpopulated spaces on its way north. The road was designed to carry men and supplies from Dawson to the oil fields on the Beaufort Sea.*

# 3
# Today

There is no boom now. In 1982, one mine after another closed because of low world prices for what Yukon mines were producing—mainly zinc, lead, silver and copper. The local economy virtually collapsed. There are still a few independent gold miners washing away entire creek valleys to recover gold, but even they see themselves threatened by tougher environmental standards proposed in the interests of salmon. For income, Yukoners are left mainly with government salaries, unemployment insurance, majestic grandeur and can-can dancing. More than ever, Yukoners rely on the wilderness and the spirit of '98 as sources of tourism revenue. Parks Canada has made Dawson a national historic site and with the help of the Yukon government refurbished a number of turn-of-the-century buildings. A highlight of the summer is Discovery Day, marking Skookum Jim's drink from Rabbit Creek. It is celebrated by people racing outhouses down the main street and drinking prodigiously from bottled beverages. It is followed by Recovery Day.

Right:
*A Yukon trapper relaxes with his pipe. The independent lifestyle of the trapper still attracts many, although fur is no longer the basis of the economy.*

Below:
*The Cogasa placer gold mine stands garishly lit against the somber landscape at 60 Mile River.*

*A pair of bored sled dogs wait for the festivities to start in Whitehorse.*

Aside from dealing with the economic slump, the main challenge to Yukoners is the same as in Alaska: to create a social system that meets the needs of native people and partly makes up for the disruptions caused by the gold rush and highway boom. The Council for Yukon Indians has been negotiating aboriginal claims with the federal and Yukon governments for several years. An agreement is predicted to benefit both native and non-native Yukoners. Natives would gain political clout and receive money collectively to establish economic ventures. Non-natives stand to gain from any new infusion of money into the territory. And the Yukon, as a place and a people, has the chance to attain the difficult balance of economic growth, wilderness preservation and maintenance of the natives' preferred way of life. It is a rare opportunity and an exciting time to be part of the North.

Opposite:
*A small plane taxies along the Porcupine River. In much of the North, these planes are the only alternative to traveling on foot.*

Above:
Lively folk art decorates an abandoned miner's cabin.

Right:
The stove inside this old trapper's cabin in the Yukon provides heat for cooking and warmth against the bitter winter cold.

Preceding pages:
As part of the Discovery Day festivities in Dawson, a young man tries to make his way up a greased pole. The holiday celebrates George Carmack's discovery of gold on August 17, 1896.

*Preparations for a long winter: cabbages for food and wood for the fire.*

135

A surveyor with the International Boundary Commission. The commission was formed to maintain and supervise the border between the United States and Canada.

Opposite:
Caribou graze on the mosses and other plants of the tundra. Herds of caribou travel across Alaska and Yukon during their migrations.

Opposite:
Bleak and rarely traveled, the Dempster Highway across Yukon was the subject of considerable controversy. Many questioned whether the project was worth the money spent and whether the road would damage the environment.

An old sternwheeler boat in Carcross, now used as a museum. The sternwheelers were once a common sight on northern waterways, but the last one was retired in the 1950s.

Bundled up for school in Faro. The town
was named after a gambling game.

A gold panner relaxes with his family
in a summer shelter.

Opposite:
The placid surface of a deep, blue lake
mirrors the Ogilvie Mountains.

Following pages:
Silhouetted against a haunting gray sky,
a man on skis pulls a sled laden with
his supplies across the barren Ogilvie
Glacier in the St. Elias Mountains.

Page 144:
The sun's rays warm the jagged peaks
of Mt. Monolith in the Tombstone
Range of the Ogilvie Mountains.